OPEN HEART

The publication of this book was supported with grants from the National Endowment for the Arts Literature and Advancement Programs, the Lannan Foundation, and the Oregon Arts Commission.

Cover art, "Internal Adjustments," by Leah Kosh.
Cover design by Cheryl McLean and Carolyn Sawtelle.
Book design by Cheryl McLean and Micki Reaman.

CALYX Books are distributed to the trade by Consortium Book Sales & Distribution, Inc., Saint Paul, MN, 1-800-283-3572. CALYX Books are also available through major library distributors, jobbers, and most small press distributors including: Airlift, Bookpeople, Inland Book Co., Pacific Pipeline, and Small Press Distribution. For personal orders or other information write: CALYX Books, PO Box B, Corvallis, OR 97339, (503) 753-9384, FAX (503) 753-0515.

∞

The paper in this book meets the guidelines for permanence and durability of the Committee on Production Guidelines for Book Longevity of the Council on Library Resources and the minimum requirements of the American National Standard for the Permanence of Paper for Printed Library Materials Z38.48-1984.

Library of Congress Cataloging-in-Publication Data

Sornberger, Judith.
    Open heart / Judith Mickel Sornberger
            p.   cm.
    ISBN 0-934971-32-3 (alk.paper): $19.95. —ISBN
0-934971-31-5 (pbk.): $9.95.
    1. Women–Poetry.   I. Title.
    PS 3569.0676506   1993
    811´.54 – dc20   93-634
                                                       CIP

Printed in the U.S.A.

OPEN HEART

Judith Mickel Sornberger

CALYX Books • Corvallis, Oregon

ACKNOWLEDGEMENTS

The author wishes to gratefully acknowledge the following
publications in which these poems were previously
published: "Angel Chimes," "Cinderella," "Night Swim in a
Farm Pond," "Packing Grandma's China," "The Place to
Begin," "Sense and Sensibility," "To a Serious Woman,"
"Women on Thanksgiving," and "Wrinkles," *Adjoining Rooms*
(Platte Valley Press, 1985); "Matriarch," *Alternatives* (Best
Cellar Press, 1986); "Night Swim in a Farm Pond," *Blue
Unicorn*, Vol. 6, No. 3, June 1983; "Knowing My Name,"
CALYX, A Journal of Art and Literature by Women, Vol. 6, No.
1, June 1981; "My Grandmother's Dolls" and "Musings in
the Garden at Poissy," *CALYX, A Journal of Art and Literature
by Women*, Vol. 8, No. 1, Fall 1983; "February Letter" and
"My Student Says She Is Not Beautiful," *CALYX, A Journal
of Art and Literature by Women*, Vol. 9, Nos. 2 & 3, Winter
1986; "Wallpapering to Patsy Cline," *CALYX, A Journal of Art
and Literature by Women*, Vol. 12, No. 3, Summer 1990;
"Dividing the Dolls" and "The Olson Women and Their
Hair," *CALYX, A Journal of Art and Literature by Women*, Vol.
14, No. 3, Summer 1993; "Pioneer Child's Doll," *City Kite on
a Wire* (Mesilla Press, 1986); "Visit," *Crossing the River: Poets of
the American West* (The Permanent Press, 1987); "Angel
Chimes," *Dear Winter* (Northwoods Press, 1984); "Women's
Aerobics Class," *Denver Quarterly*, Vol. 20/21, Nos. 4/1,
Spring/Summer 1986; "From the Art Museum's Oriental
Wing," *Denver Quarterly*, Vol. 24, No. 1, Summer 1989;
"Caprock Canyon," *Frontiers*, Vol. 10, No. 1, 1988; "Visiting
the Nation's Capital," *The Greenfield Review*, Vol. 14, Nos. 1 &
2, Winter/Spring 1987; "To a Serious Woman" and "Sense
and Sensibility," *Kalliope*, Vol. 6, No. 1, 1984; "Adam and

For my mother and father

Roberta McCord Mickel
William E. Mickel III

Contents

The medieval poet Christine de Pisan
retired to the abbey at Poissy at the age
of 55, where her daughter had taken
the veil many years earlier. One
poem remains from the time of her
seclusion—a tribute to Joan of Arc.

1. *Past all words princes wish to hear,*
   past contriving love ballades,
   past pleading with my lords for peace,
   I spend my last words on myself.

   I bow only before the sun,
   kneeling on the earth
   who welcomes me.
   I need not remind the sun
   of what it is,
   nor flatter the earth
   so she will bear her fruits.

   We three conspire in this narrow plot
   to conjure up what's needed after all:
   herbs for illness, food
   and flowers for the table.

2. *Today I prune the roses,*
   cut the dark stems at a slant
   so remembering will not be blunt
   and they will grow new, stronger limbs.

   I once used roses in my poems,
   not as they grow in gardens,

ignorant of praise, but cut
from life and held mute in the hand.
Between their layers I tucked words
to prop the petals open.

Before today their thorns were only steps
winding upward to their blooms.
But I see the roses are as proud
of straight green fingers and magenta claws
as of their unfolding faces.

Now they speak to me
in voices of their own,
not the words of poems,
but a language of open and close,
of living past the petals
falling in like withered skin.
I groom their useless parts from them.
They grow and die as they have always done.

3. *What praises can I write of my adopted land*
   when princes split her carcass
   between their traitors' teeth
   then brood over her bones
   like relics of ambitious dreams?

   Her heart fades in one coffer;
   her muscles quiver in another;
   and her thick coat is torn
   apart for purses.
   Her lesser remains are scattered,
   exposed to foreign dogs
   who, poised along our shores,
   are salivating.

My thoughts dry slowly on the page
like tears, like blood.

4. Last night I dreamed wolves killed
one of our lambs. We heard them
howling close and squeals
like fire in our ears. I dreamed
that by moonlight I found the red place
where the lamb was taken down.

Nothing else recalled the tearing,
the shrieking in the thick, dumb snow
but dark trails of blood
dripping off toward diverse lands.

5. My daughter shares this afternoon
with me on a shaded bench in the garden.
Although we sleep beneath one roof,
her work lies within, mine without.
I show her how the lettuce, beans, and peas
line up like supplicants before the sun.

She says her life inside requires a talent
for shadows. Each day dawns on the light
end of a spectrum between grey and black.
What color there is falls along the line
from morning light on dark stone walls
at matins to the absolute black
of robe and habit.

Her world variegates with women's voices.
Between alto and soprano at their prayers
she hears the whispering wings of butterflies,

dead leaves rasping in the wind,
and birdsong. All things that fall
to earth and rise beneath the sun, she says,
are in her sisters' voices.

The sun slips past the earth's black boundary.
Bells ring. I wait for her to disappear.
Still, until the last bell tolls,
I stay her hand. Now she hurries down the path.
I watch the dark reach down to touch
the edges of her robe.

6. *Eleven years I've passed in silence now.*
Whispers trickled in from former worlds,
but never loud enough to tempt my voice.
Today the name of Joan rides in
upon the feverish spring wind.
I, a bulb, sleeping in the earth's dry bed
eleven winters long, burst open
with a sudden memory of life.

While I tended cloistered gardens,
Joan was climbing up the years.
Like ivy, she stretched a delicately
tendriled mind to the sky. There St. Catherine
called her in the guise of bells.

The bells ring now in Joan's young voice.
They swell across the land like flooded streams.
Awaken, drowsy hearts of France.
Be green. We live.

My Grandmother's Dolls

Amelia Earhart Rag Doll

Into their faces I flew without grace
of feather boas, evening gowns, glass slippers.
And I wouldn't doubt a cheer went up
when the word was I'd gone down,
at least among the kind who'd say
it served me right for flying off
with some guy not my husband.

Now they've stamped me back
and front on cotton, stuffed
and stitched me in Japan
to send home in one piece, unbreakable:
the silk scarf knotted at my neck
and the sunlight glint on goggles
fixed firmly to me in this life as freckles.

I am skull of leather, jodhpurs, boots,
and mitten fingers taking hold of nothing.
Look closely: these eyes bleed
over their borders—a brazen
blue that never knew its place,
believed the sky its sister,
flew to her.

MY GRANDMOTHER'S DOLLS

Now that I am grown
and can do no further harm,
Grandma brings them out
one by one, telling me their names.
I tell Grandma I am pregnant.
She holds out her china baby doll to me.
I touch the doll's porcelain curls,
its long white muslin gown,
the lace along the hem.
I bring its cool cheek up to my own.

My mother told me once
that Grandma took care of four
younger children on the farm
until she married Grandpa.
Now, she thought, *life will finally begin.*
Six months later she was pregnant.

I hand Grandma back her doll.
For a long time she is still,
holding it against her bosom.
Then she begins rocking in her chair,
rocking and patting the doll's back.

Her eyes are pressed shut and her tears
drop onto the china baby's back.
The creak of her chair is a voice
reciting the names of the living,
the names of the dead, and they are the same
name over and over again.

Pioneer Child's Doll

Here, child, is what we mean by love:
a block head doll of coarse-grained wood,
eyes two knife-pricks, mouth a crooked stab.

As we are given to love land
that few would covet, where no tree
dares stand up to the sky,

So shall you love her whose grainsack skirt
covers, not petticoats, but sticks,
whose curls must be imagined in the wood.

And as we break the stubborn sod
of our backs to know what we
can be on this earth,

So by the sweat of your palm
on her brow will you bring
to her flat face a sheen.

French Young Lady Doll ca. 1845

Dressed in white lace *robe décolletée*,
sashed with scarlet ribbon *de velours*,
I arrived here on the plains, believing
I would dance through nights of rustling crinolines.
Sometimes I almost hear them in the sift
of leaves beneath the cottonwoods.

As my mistress matured I yearned
to trade my kidskin arms for hers
that would hold others to her softer breasts.
I traveled no more across miles, but down
through daughters' hands like tenderness itself.
I have lost little not omitted from the start:
only my satin slippers, buried in a creekbed's dust,
my long gloves forgotten two young girls ago.

I'll live as long as anyone who never lived.
The prairie sun won't split my well-cured skin.
My gray eyes will accept light
even as it drains away. My bisque face
will not bake one shade past bone.

ADAM AND EVE CLOTHESPIN DOLLS

I do not know from what tree
these two were carved. They bear
with them no fruit, no dark sweet stain.
Here smiles Eve, her wooden shoulders
filigreed with yellow curls,
one hand covering a breast.
The other hand is painted just above
the long split of her legs.

Adam does not smile.
Whoever painted his black eyes
so close together must have had
bewilderment in mind right from the start.
He holds his fig leaf with both hands,
not trusting either one alone
to hold his shame in place.
Just as neither he nor Eve was asked
to hold things up alone,
or, when the time was ripe,
to let them fall.

Pewter Angel

Where she walks no rustling is heard.
Nor will her robe's stiff pleats
cling to her knees. Starched
in something permanent as we can make it,
she is wholesome as the platter
on which rests a cut of lamb,
unyielding as armor that is her brother.

Conscripted now without regard to king
or century, he stands in a public hall,
squinting into brass and silver visors
of others who survive utility:
cocktail guests of a prankster host.

So has the angel come to stand
on a shelf in my bedroom
between a marble swan who swims
only the walnut's swirling grain
and a china mutt curled in a basket
sleeping. Relic of one dreaming
day of life when, even with lead wings,
her kind could fly, and her flameless
candle lit each of the stars.

Worry Dolls from the Natural History Museum

According to Mayan legend, when children are
troubled, one doll for each problem should be placed
beneath their pillows before falling asleep. Upon
awakening, these worries will have disappeared.

From among sharks' teeth, dinosaurs,
and magnifying cubes, my sons choose
worry dolls for souvenirs. Later
they dislodge the dolls from wooden boxes.
Some bear baskets on their heads;
others carry burdens on their backs.

Although the dolls hold out their arms,
the orange paper faces aren't friendly,
the smudged lips not the round O of surprise.
They are patient and impersonal, inviolate
as the dark inside confessionals.

The children whisper their fears
into ears they cannot see: math,
fingernail biting, big kids,
crashing on the way home.
Now I lay me down to sleep...

Is it magic, the children ask,
when dolls take away your worries?
I do not answer.

Let my children sleep
in the shadows of pyramids.
Let them whisper
to their matchstick dolls.
Let the telling be enough.

Bisque Doll Family

Pot-bellied, they stand
all of one posture: three generations
out of the same mold, all leaning
as I've seen pregnant women do
to relieve strain. But these six
are really showing off. It's the Twenties
and round bellies testify
that someone in the family's done well—
Grandpa or Papa, no doubt.

Papa, by the looks of things.
Grandpa's already nightcapped,
and Papa's wearing his top hat
at such a rakish slant, Mama
had better watch her popinjay.
But her eyes are not on Papa,
nor are they on flappers.
Her bonnet—a stew pot overturned—
is only a wee bit more in step
than Grandmother's dusting cap.

She has no time now for foolishness.
Sonny needs saving from the thousand
spills and scrapes an energetic boy
falls prey to every day. Like Papa,
he's grown smug on Mama's doting.
She can't resist his little pout,
pops a pastry between pooched-out lips,
as though he were her piggy bank
and his round tummy her proof against hunger.

Sister's easier. Her dolly is her world.
She twirls a lacy hem around one finger,
waiting for her papa to come home.
Handsome Papa, smelling of cigars
and the newspaper, will turn her
in a circle and call her his pretty bird.
I was no older than she is when my grandmother
handed down the family to me.
Good daughter, I held their pose for years,
never guessing their fragility,
never asking my mother are they a gift
that I should keep.

Dividing the Dolls

Now our mothers let us take turns choosing
dolls that we remember never touching.
Except one my sister got to dress on chilly
mornings when Mom, off to work at Mutual
of Omaha, dropped her off at Grandma's.
Jill chooses her, even though she's not
pristine or decked out like the others.

The rest of us, ruthless as pageant judges,
choose the beautiful, as we've been taught to.
I take Ireland for her emerald eyes.
Suz loves Russia's velvet cap, gold curls.
Nancy wants the creamy gaze and gleaming
nest of braids of the ceramic lady
whose bloomers, crinolines, and pin-striped
shirtwaist Grandma sewed when sharp-eyed.

We agreed it would have pleased her
to look so pretty in her dust-rose suit.
But not being handled by the strangers,
not having her arms—limp as a rag doll's—
guided through the sleeves, not her hands—
cold and rigid now as bisque—grasped
by warm hands she couldn't grasp back.
And what if her archenemy showed up and got
to act like they were still friends?

How can she lie still for the minister
quoting *Proverbs: What is a good wife?*
Remember her throwing that pail of water
down the basement stairs at Grandpa?
Remember her wanting to hire a hit-man
to take care of one of our ex's?

All the pretty dolls are gone
and there are many left to choose.
Here's a Spanish lady whose mantilla's lovely,
but doesn't cover enough of her face—so
flushed and furrowed, she's either sick
or ready to murder someone.
And a tacky hula dancer who's lost
too much of her grass skirt.
Her hair reminds us of fake shrunken heads
the boy cousins used to fight over.

Or this doll we suspect she made:
a smirk painted on her walnut head,
her hat a wilted sunflower, her feet
two wooden monsters beneath the lacy hem.
Or another creation: this tiny
ersatz Raggedy Ann, who would be cute
but for one eye embroidered huge and askew.
We can just hear her: *You see?*
I am so going blind!

These are harder to divide, harder
to claim, harder to keep
from laughing over.
Once we've broken down, we keep on
laughing till we're shaking so hard,
even our mothers can't stare us
into decent shame. Harder and harder,
till even they can't hold it in.
Till we're all rocking back and forth,
arms wrapped around our bodies
the reckless way we would
have loved her dolls once.

The Place To Begin

VISIT

Now is the time for coyotes
to stop crying in our ears;
to sell the Sandhills home
and lose the town: its cattle
history, the hills, the hills.

Grandmother leads me to the quilts
folded on her mother's bed.
One for each grandchild, our births
predicted in the heavy winters
of her mother's labor. Choose,
she says, and there are no surprises,
no new patterns: stars,
the wedding ring, log cabin.

Sure, you remember Great-grandmother,
my mother insists. I don't, and try
reading her face in the yellowed newspaper.
Obituary calls her face a china doll's.
Mom says no, she was tough.
Killed a rattlesnake trespassing
in her garden with the cane
they all believed she leaned on.

Just as they supposed her husband her support
before his cutthroat suicide in their front yard.
And she had gone on folding down the quilt
from her small body each day before dawn.
Gone on feeding children
and chickens given children's names,
gathering eggs.

I try tracing the hand that struck the snake,
its knuckles coarsened against wind and burrs,

the grit under her nails from garden work,
in the only map I have of her,
the quilt I choose: star pattern.
Here to trace her veins in tiny stitches,
here to find her hands in five-point stars.

My last night in the Sandhills
the stars come out in patterns I look for
standing knee-deep in wet pasture.
Star chart against the sky, I turn
until I'm sure north points to north,
try piecing stars into stories I hold.
But it won't work. Stars out here
are close together as quilt stitches,
close in their vast distances as relatives.
The patterns I brought with me do not fit.

Perhaps she knew those myths,
their foreign names, but chose
to give the stars an order
she inherited from women's hands,
one closer to home. Now I squint
to see them through her needle's eye,
and looking must be sharper,
less detached. It is chilly here
at night even in summer, and I fold
around myself what she has left,
knowing its warmth was not meant for me.
But in the code of stitches
my fingers read her will
to cover all she loved, and I am covered.

Matriarch

Evening's putting on her earrings,
now her loose-strung pearls.
Each night she drinks the blood
of all her rivals, the way she keeps
her complexion so high.
Now she's fastened on her opal brooch.
Good God, but she is big, big as
Great-grandmother in her dark tent smocks,
her thinning white hair floating
from her skull into the air, like stars
spreading across the Milky Way, each one
each day farther from all the others.

She ruled the atmosphere
of that house from her armchair,
too large to budge, even for meals,
glad her daughter-in-law saw
to all that now. Let her play
lady-of-the-house. Her own life
had been the backdrop for each breath
taken, each word spoken in that house
as long as anyone remembered.
When my grandmother delivered
her tray to the living room, we sitting
at the table in the next room held
our breath to hear her blunt approval.

My sisters and I sat up to the crystal
goblet table in our Christmas satin,
like ornaments sewn to a gown
no one would dare wear. Not even
Great-grandmother, whose hand had drawn

the pattern, seemed to care
what perfect ladies she had spawned.
She was beyond us, in the next room,
the ticking of her fork the only signal
through our lively chatter that she lived.

Until Grandmother rose, as if on cue,
as if some message reached her from beyond
light years, by radar only her pearl-
seeded ears could be sensitive to,
and left the dining room. When she returned,
the half-empty dish told us the news:
cratered mashed potatoes in a crescent
harbored a constellation of new peas.
Enough food left to say her appetite
was waning, enough gone to say
she'd not give it up yet.

The Place To Begin

for a mother-in-law

The place to begin is not your death
nor my divorce. It is not the priest-
less wedding of your Catholic son
to a Protestant. Perhaps the best place
is in the kitchen where you stand
before me now in memory.

You teach me to dice vegetables
all so uniform no one would guess
they've come from things as varied
as carrots and potatoes. Romaine
lettuce leaves are delicate as baby
skin and must be laid to dry
on white linen tea towels.

Half a glass of red wine in your hand,
you sauté the vegetables, giggling
over some silliness between us.
When you laugh so hard tears come
and you remove thick-lensed glasses
to wipe your eyes, still laughing, I see
the young woman you must have been,
striking out for a California modeling
career in defiance of your mother.

My guess is that since the first day
of your firstborn you've been waiting
for the slap your mother smarted with
the day you left, for, as we cook,

the things that you refuse to know
about your own children are everywhere
but in our talk: my being on The Pill;
Cathy's living in sin with her boyfriend;
David's fighting with his wife.

While the sauce thickens, you show me
the landscape you're working on.
Like your make-up and your hair,
your paintings are faithful
to magazine photographs. Grasping
hairbrush or paintbrush, your hands
are the devotion of a manuscript
illuminator painting again and again
someone else's vision.

Beside each dinner plate you place
a cup of vitamins especially selected
for each person. You are always
on the watch for pale complexions,
dark-ringed eyes, and listlessness
you have faith vitamins will cure.

Yesterday your son told me
that in your last five years
the fears you never allowed yourself
had one by one come home to you:
your oldest daughter, Laura, dead—
your happy child, the one who watched
for hours as you put just the right
light in the sky; other divorces;

your husband's desertion;
your youngest daughter, Mary,
pregnant at fifteen.

I want to believe
that the children who had trailed
away from all you were
faded in your last months
as you watched this daughter's belly rise,
that you could almost ignore
what grew in your own breast,
that you could almost feel
the child's head resting there,
solid, absolute.

Open Heart

Tomorrow my grandmother meets her faith
at knifepoint in the dark
center of her apostate heart.

She squirms in the short, dust-white gown
to think of being cut and folded back,
her heart's weakness betrayed to the light.

Once a neighbor girl taught me the *Our Father*.
My prize for remembering, a carnival-bright card,
revealed a woman draped in blue.
Her heart wept scarlet drops.

I ran terrified at what I carried,
burrowed beneath a rosebush, buried her.
Then I pricked my palms
until she washed away.

I can't tell my grandmother this story.
She would take it as revulsion at her pain.
How to tell her I'm still running,
out of breath with shame?

Not her shame in suffering the honest
losses of the body, but that of coming to her
bearing roses and a card, refusing,
as the afternoon goes gray, to bare my fear.

As I leave she takes my hand, whispers
pray for me. An unbeliever, I nod anyway:
If you promise to live.
Probably we've made a pact neither can keep.

But I'll not repent as long as there's a chance
I'll learn to open my heart wide as hers.
To open it as she has always done,
against the odds.

Poem in September, on My Mother's Birthday

You've come for a visit, and it's snowing.
I am flowing heavy in the way your body
taught me. You say you're still spotting,
your body not yet willing
to forget its favorite story.

I want to show you mountains,
but you haven't brought the right clothes
for this weather. I dress you
in old boots, unmatching mittens,
and a scarf that we say, laughing,
makes you look like Red Riding Hood.

Beside a slim canal, we walk through woods.
Before we're halfway to the clearing
you need to stop and catch your breath.
I notice then how doggedly
age breathes down your throat,
so I contrive reasons for us to dawdle.

You tell me Grandma's growing dotty,
mixes stories up. Last week she told
you of her childhood Christmas
without dolls. You hadn't heart
to tell her she had been the mother,
you the doll-less daughter.

For years she's been collecting dolls,
so many of them in her house
there's hardly room to sit down
when we visit. Mother, lately I've seen

dolls collecting in your house.
You fire the heads and limbs.
Your mother stuffs their trunks
and petticoats them.

Telling me this story as we walk
has chopped your breath to pieces.
You would like to sit down.
Why don't I go on, and you'll catch up.
But wait, the woods have opened
like a giant picture book to let us see
far off into the distance.

Like you now, the mountains wear
a thick mantle of snow. The air hangs
heavy with the breathing of the wolf.
Mother, this is not the view
I brought you here to see:
both of us are on the way to Grandma's;
whoever walks ahead, you'll get there first;
the woodcutter is up there on the hillside
felling trees for cottage after cottage.

Packing Grandma's China

*You'd be surprised how little
you need,* Grandma assures, tearing
newspaper squares smaller than
the plates. *Honey, if you only knew
all the times I've packed dishes.*
Her hands fold over paper on her lap,
and she tells about the time they moved
when she was eight months pregnant
(*with you, Roberta,* inclining
her head sideways at my mother).

Her eyes stare into the glass
gaze of a china cabinet pane.
*You'd think that crackerbox
was a palace we were so tickled.*
My mother takes over the tearing
(her squares more generous) as Grandma
recites street names and houses' colors,
angry again at the sewer men who
trampled her flower bed on Ruggles—
daisies, marigolds, and pansies
she'd started from seed. When she
called the city, *some scalawag
asked how much damage was done.
In dollars and cents, he says.
Can you imagine?*

They were always moving to a little
bigger house until the kids moved out.
When Grandpa died she rented an apartment.
She thinks it foolish keeping
that extra bedroom, his narrow cot.

She worries, though, that the new place
will not hold everything. *I guess
I'll set whatever won't fit in the middle
of the living room and see
what I get sick of first.*

She offers me salt shakers, a cake plate,
and a book of Swedish recipes. *Roberta,
you might as well take the silver.
That way you can use it for Thanksgiving.*
We open the wooden box to touch
the tarnished spoons, but when she sees
them tangled on red velvet, she snatches
it away. *Now, how'd they get like that?*

We watch her fit each piece
into its slot, letting her white
fingers slide along the rose-
carved stems. We are not allowed
another peek before she shuts
the lid and fastens it.

My mother puts the box in the back seat,
and we drive, silent, through red oaks.
In one yard an old man kneels.
He brings his arms under the pile of leaves
and holds them to his chest like the body
of someone he loves. My mother stops
at the corner, bows her head over the wheel.
Oh Jude (she calls me by my childhood name),
I didn't want to take the silver.

KNOWING MY NAME

*Judith of Bethulia was a Hebrew
widow who saved her people on
the eve of battle by seducing
Holofernes, the Assyrian general,
and cutting off his head.*

She may pretend
she has never heard
of Judith of Bethulia,
but my mother will never deny
that she raised me
like a favorite weapon
to fly against the wind.

Just as surely as she knows
that cardinals flickering against
the snow like feathered garnets
in her backyard are there
intentionally on a day when her eyes
think gray the only color possible,

my mother named me
to slash through gray,
to saunter into the enemy's tent
with a sword keened
on her love for me,
lusting for something red.

The Naming of Sara Rebecca

for Cathy

The book of your fathers teems with second chances:
Sarah spent all her days barren until God told
Abraham his seed would blossom in her womb
that had been dry for decades. Within the tent
Sarah overheard, could not help laughing: *After
I have grown old and my husband is old, shall I
have pleasure?* Her laughter swelled the tent walls,
lifted through a flap—a laugh of pure delight,
not doubt. But God misunderstood and stamped his foot:
Is anything too hard for the Lord?

Cathy, we've know men like that. We've known
so many men, a listing of their names would surpass
all the begats of the Scriptures. After our divorces
we coupled like Noah's good daughters-in-law
on drying land. So we made love without loving.
Where is love's name among the generations?
And where are the fruits of those unions?
How could we let them flourish, having produced
in love three sons between us?

Then we took second husbands the same summer, dared
another taste of sun-ripe olives, and the seed
you'd buried like a secret in the desert came to flower.
Once women of our season were told not to conceive,

before science and the law allowed a woman to refuse
fruit bruised within her. My own tubes tied,
I watch my last chance for a daughter rise in you,
perhaps as Sarah contemplated Hagar's rising belly:
with some envy and some hope of sharing.

Your daughter will be called Sara Rebecca
for two strong women of the Torah, women like us
who have survived, not because we took new husbands,
but because we nursed within us the parched pit
of the olive—a tree capable of self-pollination,
of regeneration from a dried-up stick.
Sara she shall be: our one survivor,
our proof of power sprouting in the desert.

The Olson Women and Their Hair

It matters that Grandma's looks pretty
on the eyelet pillow. We all say
how soft the perm looks,
know that in a slightly lighter sleep
she'd put a hand up, squeeze the curls,
and ask us, *Do you think so?*

Her younger sister, Maxine, can't come
to the funeral. Right in the middle
of a chemo cycle, she won't let us
visit, can't stand us seeing
how terrible my hair looks.
Thank God she isn't losing it,
we say, meaning her hair.

We cousins use Grandma's currency, exchange
hair stories: horrors, compliments,
and complications. The way some families
discuss disease, birth, and business.
Aunt Gloria approves my sister's haircut.
Bobbed to the chin, it makes her face fuller.
Mom doesn't like it, Jill announces.
I said it looked very smart, Mom protests.
Jill laughs: *Just not pretty!*

Mom remembers Gloria's giving me
a perm on my first birthday.
They get out the pictures and I wince
to see my hair: thinner than Grandma's
in the coffin. You can see
the sky through every curl.

Suz says Grandma taught her how to tease
her hair, the way she'd poufed herself

from farm girl into flapper.
Gloria had not approved, thought she
should sit still for another Toni.

With her mother in the room,
Nancy won't bring it up, but we remember
Gloria's forcing her to wear a headband
all through senior high. As if her yellow
curls falling freely would turn her
too soon into a woman, fallen.

Nancy hates that hers is the only
hair that never changes. Even though,
at thirty, she has stood up
for the first time to her mother,
her hair lies docile as a good dog.

Suz and I—the oldest girls—have taken
different roads to middle age.
Suz's darkness touched with red tones,
cut short like the girl-huntress, Diana's.
Mine's gone from chin to shoulders,
trying to recall its youth, even
its much earlier blondeness.

We have come to bury the dead,
but Grandma's name will come up
as long as we have hair
to fuss with, cut, or cuss.
As long as we love what we hate
and never stand for loss.

Caprock Canyon

Where earth throws open her ledgers
to the sky's eternal audit,
we sisters walk beside husbands,
each trailing two children,
for once achieve a balance,
though delicate as that of sand to soil,
of rain to drought, turning the cactus
blossom red, starflower white
beneath one sunset; precarious
as our steps on the ledge to see more deeply.

The earth's a faithful bookkeeper,
displays in honest layers
all her losses, every river
forced between her thighs,
white caprock holding trinkets
each has offered: little lives
that crumbled when she pressed
them to her breast, whose shapes—
her souvenirs—she cradles still.

Our own mother likes working with figures.
At the family planning clinic
she can make things come out even:
on one side, the women overcome
with the red caves of children's mouths,
and on the other side, services rendered.
Perhaps she too was overcome

when our births came so close together.
How she must have labored
to balance her attentions.

You and I spread our shared childhood out
between us in the evening—a crazy
quilt to make sense of together,
the way we used to count the stars
from sleeping bags as children,
dividing the night into equal sectors.
We're tallying the favors given
to each daughter, counting scraps
of silk and velvet, humble muslin—
each of us determined to uncover
errors calculated in the other's favor.

By the time we have unstitched
each threadbare segment, the stars
have faded from the night sky's pattern,
and we're enemy camps around the same
dying fire without a cover.
Children once more, we count on sleep
to restore warmth, and on the even
breathing of our children, their dream
struggles mercifully screened from us.

The thing we'll wake to first
will be the canyon, our chill
standing divided in its shadow.
Then, one by one, the sun

will light the eras, until—gorgeous—
they're a coat of many colors:
gold, maroon, and gray—each telling
its own story:
                erosion
                        dissolution
        disappearance

all sharing one inheritance
with neither grief nor envy.

VISITING THE NATION'S CAPITAL

Each day I visit the Mary Cassatt
mother and daughter in the spring
of that delicate love affair:
the girl reclining in her mother's lap
old enough to know her mother's beauty,
just old enough to see in the hand mirror
reflections of it on her own round cheeks.

I've seen the women strolling by
hold small daughters to that spot,
wait for them to lean against their thigh.
I've heard them murmur to their daughters,
seen the edges of their interlacing fingers
go fuzzy the way Cassatt paints
women's hands sometimes.

This is while their congressmen
are putting their hands
up for the MX.

Down the hall Madonnas never leave
off their adoring, their hands crossed
over breasts, painting after painting
of one attitude, and the others,
holding holy children on their laps,
guarded by the wise-looking,
uniformed Black men of Washington
in the cool, still weather monitored
in a central office to prevent
their skin flaking off.

Their narrow-lidded eyes give them
the look of Oriental princesses.
I recall Japanese dolls
a few buildings down, sent to us
after the war as friendship tokens:
a bisque girl and her brother
in traditional kimonos. We keep them
behind glass for their protection.

How long before we really know
how fragile these things are,
before we learn to keep
the dolls out in the open
and not break them? Dolls
the Japanese call *ningyo*
meaning "human form."

In the rare book vault
I see books five hundred years old,
one with illuminations on white vellum:
a Madonna, child, angels in scarlet,
blue and gold-leaf on the skin
of a calf that died to make a missal
its makers believed would ensure life.

I learn how books get undone
and dipped in water to lose acids,
how they are brought up sodden
and smoothed out, given new life.
I love whoever baptizes the paper
in this way, for the adoration

of the word it takes to repeat
something so tedious with care.
And the one who heals the holes
by grafting on the strong,
transparent paper hand-made in Japan.

Coming up out of the dark
into an early spring, I almost believe
there is a cure for everything,
even for what's going on a few blocks off,
where funding for the MX will be approved today
by what some will call a comfortable margin.

All right, I am naive
like the art of an earlier America
that doesn't represent the depths of things.
But I have to believe
in the surface of things first,
in the thin layer of life over this city.

If only I could take this city
at face value, this city where diplomats
convene behind Greek pillars,
where busy streets are lined with cherry trees
from Japanese silkscreens, blooming their hearts out,
and where the art of all ages,
nations, rival schools cohabits
in one peaceable kingdom.

This city, allegory of repair and preservation,
makes me want to believe we will learn
not only to restore what has been damaged,
not only to protect whatever's fragile,
but also to control the careless flailing
of our arms, to use the hands of mothers
when our hands touch anything.

CINDERELLA

CINDERELLA

One sister cut off her toe,
another, part of her heel.
My sister seemed to lose nothing,
marching at eighteen toward the first
boy who would choose her from the others,
the first to call her eyes blue stars.

She depends now on strangers
for that version of herself.
Leaving home for the evening,
her breasts forget her son's recent mouth,
her lips, the husband's dry kiss.

The smokey bar awakens her nipples.
Alert through the lace of her blouse,
they spot a set of admiring eyes.
A smile opens wide her face.
There is always one who finds some mention
of himself in the sway of her hips,
and together they dance through
the long jazz of the night.

At midnight she eludes him and rushes
home to collapse into her cinder bed.
If she forgets anything in these bars,
she never misses it, exchanging
one amnesia for another. Whatever
she leaves behind is never recognized
as hers, nor is it ever used to trace her
to a story that ended long ago.

Wallpapering to Patsy Cline

for my mother and sister

We're here to cover the cracks
in the wall, to forgive the bad
taste of previous owners, to bury
the orange and brown daisies in a service
transforming this home into yours, sister.
We don't drywall or drive nails,
but, like our mother's mother, a good seamstress,
we know how to make an offcast
garment fit our wishes. We form
a procession we've practiced before,
kitchen to dining room, this time bearing
drop cloths, utensils, dutch ovens of paste.

Patsy sings us through some stripping:

>   *I*
>   *fall*
>   *to*
>   *piec-*
>   *es....*

a tune we know too well. We work
as when my ballerinas, your floral stripes,
and Mom's teacup scenes met in the hallway's
neutral eggshell. There are too many generations
of wallpaper here to strip. We stop
when we come to fully petalled cabbage roses.

Patsy says she has to choose today
between a poor man's roses

and a rich man's gold.
Choose the gold, we're yelling,
giddy in the futility of warning.
We're brushing bubbles to the bottom, giggling,
but they won't be brushed away,
and we find they're buried
under the old paper, an error made
so far back we can't hope to mend it.
Choose the gold, Patsy,
and buy yourself some roses.

And now she loves him

so - o - o - o

much

it hurts her,

a sob in her voice we recognize,
having heard it often in each other's.
But Mother, Sister, *deep within my heart*
lies a melody, one that doesn't twang
with regret. Patsy's right,
we need some loving too.
Yes, we do.
Indeed we do.
You know we do.

But look at the room we've created:
pastels of triangles, lovers' triangles—
but not in that old, stripped-down usage.
Think of them as pyramids, homes to hold us
forever, a woman at each angle.

JUDITH BEHEADING HOLOFERNES

When the artist Artemisia Gentileschi
was raped by her artist-father's
collaborator (who also stole one of the
old man's Judiths), *Pere Gentileschi*
filed charges, but nothing came of them.

Praise the god in broad forearms—
these women at their work:
the turbaned maidservant in muslin,
Judith glowing in brocade, her delicately
patterned sleeves rolled above the elbow
for the chore of pulling a sword
blade through a thick man's throat.

In this dark tent the maid hovers
over Holofernes, holding one arm down,
while the other reaches for her face
with knotted fist—her chin, forehead
patient as a Madonna's.

Judith braces herself, one flexed arm
against the head, his beard writhing
like worms between her fingers. Stern-
jawed as her god, she inflicts on him
her faith in the necessity of pain.
No cry spurts from her victim's throat,
only strands of blood to rival gold-set
rubies braceleting her arm.

Let Artemisia's *Judith* announce
her own revenge, not only on her rapist—
the man whose wrinkled forehead begs

the viewer's mercy—but on her father
and others who painted Judith dainty,
coy, surprised by the already severed head.
Let her revenge come slowly as it was revealed
to Holofernes on her canvas:
with measured strength
and fully relished method.

FEBRUARY LETTER

Dear Mother,
my mother-in-law
bled all January,
her spirits below zero
through the long Dakota winter.
Her son, who stayed
her bleeding once
for a period of months,
has moved south
and can't think
how to help her.
The lithium no longer works,
or anti-depressants.
She thinks she should go off
it all, but the doctor's
recommending shock again.

Mother, my soother,
apothecary of my first blood-
summer, what can a daughter
not of her blood do
when spring will not return
for months, and some things
never do?

You say your own law-mother
tells of hunching over dish water
each night for years, dropping
tears into its dark, not knowing
why. It took losing her uterus
to bring her to the surface,

and she rose clear
as her mother-in-law's crystal
when she dried it, but broken
in a way no one could see,
like the chipped pieces she kept
at the back of the buffet.

Mother, I will never prescribe
loss of any part,
I, who took her son,
her heart, her dearest blood;
I, who have sons to lose
and my own blood running out.
I can only write to her:
Come visit us.
The cardinals you loved here
are returning just in time
to show against the last
swatches of snow.

Sense and Sensibility

Jane Austen could have written the beginning:
Grand-dad, a dapper young gent from the city,
meets your brother hunting in the country
near your home (except here the city is Omaha,
the country, western Nebraska,
your home, a cattle ranch).

Your brother brings him home
and from your place at dinner
you smile a girl's flirtation
with the mystery of distance.
Your walks with him around the grounds
are viewed as an engagement.
Your father makes some inquiries,
and, finding his connections suitable,
your mother begins sewing your trousseau.

If only it had ended there
with Grand-dad transporting you
in comfort to his family home
where Austen wisely leaves us every time.

You too must have been surprised
that it went on from there.
When three children came
in that many years, did you forget
that there had ever been another you,
another him, or any other story?
Cramped beneath his parents' roof
between the nursing of his mother
and the meals you cooked for seven,

did you ever wander back to the beginning,
to the wider skies that promised everything?

When the family sewing machine business
failed, you sewed dresses for the fashionable
matrons, who, each time they dropped by
for a fitting, recalled aloud the parties
Grand-dad's mother gave: waiters,
champagne on the lawn, Japanese lanterns.
Meanwhile, Grand-dad sat out the remainder
of his life in the Starlight Bar & Grill.

And, being by that time Austen's
sensible Elinor more than you ever were
her flighty Marianne, you never even sighed
as you sewed me at eighteen
into my wedding gown.

My Student Says She Is Not Beautiful

Who was it said
you are not beautiful
to her, and flowers are.
Who was it
created the chart
ranking roses at the top,
all others under.
So that she would say
before us all,
the old men at the home
followed her
down their gray corridors
not because I'm pretty,
I am not,
but because the flowers
are her job.

Who was it told
the old women
only youth is lovely,
and flowers, and someone
else must do the choosing.
So that they too
followed her cart
on legs that barely walk,
as if on it rode
beauty missed or lost,
each one fighting
through the crowd
to clutch her sleeve:
Are they for me?
I know the roses are for me.

Wrinkles

On a line under one eye
three small dark birds have landed.
Their claws marry the wire.
They hold to this wintery perch
as I hold to a face developing
into an alien landscape.

Perhaps someday I will be
grateful for whatever I can hold,
even for the cruel things—
the network of lines crossing my face,
birds gathering there for a song
that, at twenty, I never could have heard.

WOMEN'S AEROBICS CLASS

I say I exercise
to keep my heart in shape,
but who sees the shape of my heart?

I alone account for my heart's work,
count the beats broadcast to wrist
and throat, compare my rate
to others on a table.

The heart requires high activity
for fifteen minutes straight
to keep it fit. We kick,
punch, lunge our quick
responses to hard beating
music wailing love.

Now we are down on the floor
to lift our legs, to scissor
open, shut. We are shaping
hips and buttocks that invite—
what? Or, we are building thighs
that know how to repulse,
calves that power flight
from a pursuer.

But on our backs, knees bent, we pulse
our pelvises toward the beat.
Now squeeze, comes the command.
Make it burn. We make it
burn. We are burning.
We have moved like this before,

delivering pleasure, then
life on a table.

Then we come back for more,
to feel our bodies
ache with healing, to shape up:
Sit-ups where we push
our heads and shoulders through
legs raised and spread
to bear the bodies
of ourselves alone, to level
the mound that love,
departed, left.

Trying on Swimsuits with Mother: Memorial Day

Round and round the rack I go,
the rack that reads *Size 12,*
for all to see where I belong
having neglected and eaten my way here;
oh yes, and my other flaw:
having gone around another year.

Here, Mother, your word for me,
voluptuous, is obsolete. *Sleek*
is the look the sales clerk
wants to help me fit into.
Without a snicker, she asks
my figure problems. I point
to breasts and hips. *Too large,*
I am confessing, so she, another
woman, whose eyes are better trained
than God's for detecting deceit,
will not have to pass judgment on them.

Your waist is small, she offers,
mercifully. *Let's try a wraparound.*
Accentuate and downplay is our credo.
My arms are full of black, but you
shove a clutch of bright colors at me.
Black is slimming, you admit,
but stripes will call attention to my curves.

Each year I disappear behind this curtain,
face my flesh under blue lights,

and each year what they reveal
to me is clearer. I remember
when bikinis couldn't reveal enough,
when you warned: *Dad won't let you
out in that.* What pride I took
in what I had to hide.

Bikinis gave way to a maillot
after the twins' birth, but always
I believed I could go back
to them. The clerk is bringing in
the suits with little skirts,
the kind I swore I would never wear.
But thank God you are urging me
to go the other way, showing me
a French-cut that gives away more thigh,
an optical illusion to add length.
This season we know I need illusions.

The time has come to choose
between the Speedo tank in black
and a neon stripe cut low
both front and back.
Are the stripes too youthful?
But you grin: *Do I need to slap you?
When did you start talking like that?*
We decide on stripes, but at the checkout
I can see you're troubled. I pay,

we walk outside, and I'm surprised
and grateful it's still daylight.

You wince in the sun and turn to me:
You're still a little girl,
and don't forget it.
We smile and I watch wrinkles
radiate from your sunglasses,
and in their glare my own
wrinkles' reflection. I see
how I've betrayed you: outgrowing
first our years of fitting struggles,
and then my lean bikini body.

Mother, did you foresee this day,
mourn it in advance, that day
my length no longer fit
the curve of your young-mother's arm?

THE FIRST, SECOND, AND LAST SCENE OF MORTALITY

a needle picture by Prudence Punderson

Silk stitch leads to silk stitch
as one day to another,
as cradle leads to coffin.
On my left, cradle-bound,
the baby sleeps, her hands facing
one another on the quilt I tied—
yarn sprouting in neat rows
across white cotton.

Across the carpet woven
square by square from our own wool,
a coffin rests on the oak drop-leaf
table. Precise as nails, I bordered
its lid in white French knots,
and with the same staccato stitch,
scrolled my initials like twin
constellations in the center
of black satin.

Within the fringed circumference
of carpet, seated between one
sleep and another, I work
with fabric, pen, and rule,
outlining my pattern:
a stem, a leaf, another leaf.

The Absence of Color

My mother wears black well.
So does her daughter. Changing
for the evening, she goes from black
knit cowl to beaded black angora,
so strong is her black habit.
What does she need of color?
She creates effects more various
from silence than most can hear
in the entire chromatic scale.

Widows and nuns and concert musicians
wear black. It doesn't matter
if it flatters them or not.
Poets performing don black dresses:
Listen: I am not a poetess.
Sexton and Kumin passing back
and forth the same black dress
like a consecrated garment,
a shared habit: refusing
to flinch from any darkness.

The women poets I know flirted
with wearing the habit, not to become
Christ's brides, but to find some work
that could be done—some dark
corner to illuminate in just one lifetime.
Now they live in the narrow cells of poems,
disciples of the word.

My mother taught me language—
tones for getting what I wanted,
no tone absent: coaxing, plaintive,
fierce—I've played them all
in all their combinations.
Have I gotten what I want yet?
Let me take a peek here in the closet.
Here are the rows of color, the promis-
cuity of my intentions, and the white
gown that promised me the presence
of all color. But now I want to sing
the words she taught me *par exemplum:*
I am a woman—serious, alone.

She is a woman who knows her own beauty.
She doesn't wear black like a nun.
She wears it to set off, not hide,
her auburn hair; to bring up, not wash
out, her face's colors. She's never had
her "colors done." She won't sit still
for someone saying, "Winter is your season.
Wear melon, emerald, fuschia. Avoid neutrals."

A woman choosing black says I am not
ripe fruit to sweeten up your palate.
I am not a gem to sparkle on your left arm.
Nor am I a flower—not rose, not violet,

not marigold—to press and fade, forgotten
between pages someone else wrote.

I do not live a day or two and die.
I survive the dawn's chiffon fashion parade,
and the sunset's firey striptease.
Black says I will even survive love—
its first blush, its blue periods, its absence.
Black says I will dive into the dark well
of my throat and come up singing.

Women Who Dream of Men

ANGEL CHIMES

In a few days Christmas will descend
on them, bearing the usual burden
of breakable wonder, but tonight
she and her sons will walk to the store
to buy candles for the angel chimes.

When they return to their dark house,
they will awaken the Christmas tree's
blinking eyes, take turns lighting
the slim white candles. And she,
who no longer believes, will believe
anything this close to Christmas.

The angels will wear the offering
of light upon their wings.
They will follow one another
around the central star
in a circle born entirely of light.

The song of their turning
will tingle over the woman's skin.
The children will be silent,
turning in their own orbits.
This close to Christmas
she will believe
they will never turn away.

CONFIRMATION

Drenched in the same waters,
brought up pure,
Ed Leach and I believed
ourselves early betrothed.
After all, we were the stars
of baptism class that spring
the bees toiled, busy as sin
outside our tower window
that the sun entered
shy as a first kiss,
pre-cleansing us with light.

Now, one in the body
of Christ, we sat at the foot
of the altar, our heads
in the high priests' hands.
And as they gave my soul
to God, I felt the presence
of his thigh beside mine
and looked forward to the next
rungs on the sacramental ladder
in our manual: marriage
and the laying on of hands.

When the long droning prayer
had run out, the room filled
with an anthem and we marched
together down the aisle
back to our parents to partake

of grape juice and little cubes
of Wonder Bread, like the tea parties
my sisters and I served neighbor boys.
Oh, small taste, small sip,
morsel of what's to come.
I wanted more.

WISH

Feeling dark and exotic
after the day of sun
I sit with you on the bank
of a man-made lake in Kansas,
wishing it were the Nile,
wishing we were eating something
other than potato chips—
figs, perhaps, or olives.

I wish the stars
would come out with it:
To which do I owe
my skin and skeleton,
the cloaks I wrap
around my longings?
And to which do I owe
my silver hair?

When we speak of my children,
I wish they were here
and that they'd never been born.
I wish I were sitting beside you
with all things still before me,
that my children were still
grains of light we could awaken
in the tunnels of this night's sleep.

I wish that you could come to me
tonight with any other yardstick
but the past, and that the past

had not been the only way here.
I wish I would become worthy of stars.
I wish you could forget the darkening
sky and admit that just for now
there is no other moon
than the one bobbing on my hair.

Look, you say, pointing to the drop
of light newly fallen from the moon's
wan face, *the first star.*
Make a wish.

Night Swim in a Farm Pond

Once the black sky
thickened with stars
and our clothes fell
in sudden patterns
on the hard-packed dirt.
Fireflies splashed
the water gold.

Before we wrinkled
the pond's wide face,
stars murmured over it
like the mouths of fish.
But when we dove in,
the long, dark memory
of water swallowed
in one gulp
their distinct voices.

I lay on my back
in the cool water,
the crisp stars of the sky
pricking my skin.
Ears below the surface,
I listened for traces
of the sunken stars
and took the low humming
I heard for their moans
rising from silt
that held them.

Tonight you lie in darkness
over me, covering my body
like the sky, constellations
freckled on your shoulder
near my face.

I will listen
for what lies
under me always.
I will never unhear
the particular voices
of what has been driven
beneath this present,
beneath your hands
moving over my skin
like the cool light
of stars on water.

Stained Glass

for my sister
Christmas Eve, 1985

One of Michael's windows hangs between us
and the darkness, its one red eye a blind clot.
You're telling me your recurring dream:
the bell rings; through the storm-door's glass
he proclaims himself alive, his drowning a lie.
His blood, he promises, still courses
through his body, connecting all his organs,
like the leading in his windows holding
colored shapes to his design. His face
has all its color. You believe him.

Your face drains with the telling.
From his sleep your son sends up a whimper,
like a bubble bursting on the surface
of the pond his dad went under.
Each time you try seeing Michael's face now,
you're straining through the muddy
moss-strewn water, a pane so opaque
no light will travel through it.

His paid work was restoring churches' windows,
putting back a fallen halo, replacing
the cracked pink feet of apostles.
While he made them whole, did he believe them holy?
Now is the darkest time,
the season for believing.
As the candles sputter toward extinction,
we borrow phrases from the speech

you gave your son before the funeral,
try mixing them with splinters
of carols he sang this evening.

The stars are brightly shining.
But they are far away, too far
to give us new light in our lifetime.
We say someone *so tender and mild* must be,
though we can't see him, shining somewhere.
But no light solders cut glass over your head
into an aureole as confirmation.
The blues, gold, and the roses
his hands joined are joined to darkness.

As I put out the tapers you tiptoe
to where your boy lays down his sweet head.
And though we cannot say we know
the stars look down where he lies,
God rest you, sister, in this brief absence
of color; and tomorrow, for the child's sake,
let nothing you dismay, though memory takes
its diamond blade across your face,
and each smile you make is a crack
beginning.

FIRE AND ICE

At the cemetery Mom can't keep her mind
on the praises sung her mother.
All she can think about is lifting up
the astro-turf dropcloth to peek
under the coffin: What if there's
been some mistake? Will she have
to make them dig a new hole?
Last year Grandma almost died to find
another woman buried near her husband.
She made Mom promise she'd be wedged between them.

Ever since I was a little girl
they slept in separate rooms.
Grandma kept her bedroom cool.
But air conditioning gave Grandpa sinus.
Even as kids we knew they fought.
Little phrases drifted from our mothers'
mouths like fallout to our ears:
locked doors, a pail of cold water,
someone's crying. *He was awful
stubborn, that man. But so handsome,*
she'd say with pride after he died.
More than once she'd had to elbow
some fresh gal out of the picture.

Put a Swede and an Irishman together,
the cousins say, shaking their heads,
fire and ice, fire and ice.
So that's what we are made of.
That and this earth, home of both

hearth-fire and deep-freeze.
Where oppositions melt into one river.
A convert to Grandpa's faith,
Grandma commanded us
to put our faith in God.

But thank God no one's saying,
Now she is with Grandpa, meaning Heaven.
If we believe one thing
it's that her heaven is his bones:
that handsome devil all her own
again, sleeping next door.

Lamp Man

I won't say he was our guiding light,
not a beacon pointing out the way,
not a beam of light flooding the face.
He was there more like a star, grand
and romantic in his far-off way,
but still something to steer by:
part of the constellation of wild-west
stories his family immortalized
itself in, one of the mirror lights
by which we daughters saw our faces.

I kept praying he would see the light.
He'd drive us to church, but wouldn't step
a foot inside, said any criminal could go
to church, but would that make him a nice guy?
He believed in his ability to sell,
but even that he never gambled on
until we were gone. Then everything went
into lamps, a van, and being his own boss.

Now that the family farm is dying out
in Kansas, Iowa, Nebraska, what small town
dealers still exist aren't buying,
but that won't stop the lamp man.
Where a blue-winged angel couldn't sell
the word of God for wishes, he bears
his lamps. Reliable as sunlight, he sweeps
across his territory, horizon to horizon,
Ogallala to Oskaloosa in one day.

He's got in a new line—touch-tone control—
a new way to fill the houses
they're about to lose with light.
They're his offering, their consolation
prize for everything they worshipped
having turned indifferent to their touch,
their pleading. When I visit he sits reading
under one of his own lamps
while my mother and I bow heads
in an unlit corner, and I confess
my many fears and losses.

I do not tell him my secrets or wishes.
I do not say I am more godless than he
was in his non-observance. In his presence
I am silent as I am walking alone under stars.
But each time I leave he offers me another lamp,
its gold neck gleaming sword-like in his grasp,
as if to say, *For you, daughter, there cannot be
enough light. For you I would vanquish all darkness.*

My Twin Sons Talk with Me about Survival

Robinson Crusoe, one son says,
washed up on his island
more dead than alive.
Each time he tells the story differently,
emphasizing once which animal he killed
to make his boots and another time
what foods he feasted on, but each telling
requires the phrase *more dead than alive,*
as though the struggle wasn't with the sea
or with the wilds, but in the man himself.

My other son talks of the Kalahari.
Stranded there without water or food,
he'd cut a cactus open, drink the juice.
His teacher says she'd kill
an animal and drink the blood.
He believes she would, and wants to know
if I'd do the same.
If it were the difference between life...
I start to say, but he stops me:
It's okay, Mom, it'll never happen.

Yet, regularly as a pulse, they ask me
to retell the story of their early births:
how no one expected them to live but I,
and even I more demanded than expected it.
The part they won't let me omit
is how I cried the first time
I stood beside their isolettes,
how I couldn't breathe watching
their chests puff up and deflate

like sails ragged in a storm.
I think they believe in the tears
of that story or in the stubbornness
more than they do in the blood
the doctor sent into their fevered night
with a cargo of oxygen and no message of hope.

A CLASH OF BONE: A PAINTING OF PACHYCEPHALOSAURI

for my twin sons

When you were discovering your bones
buried in the genes' prehistory, evolving
from tadpoles swimming in one pond
to uncurling otters, I felt the fight
begin under my heart—the kick,
the kicking back, the elbowing out of the way.
You kicked each other out too early,
lungs fishy still, and when you lived
past the doctor's expectations,
he shook his head: "They're fighters!"

Maybe your water-ballet boxing match
prepared you for life on this hostile planet,
for you pulled yourselves through
when no mama's mammal warmth, no blood
transfusion promised you a future.
Now, at twelve, you struggle to hatch
hairy, rumbling-throated creatures
from the bodies of my babies, a fight
none of us has trained for. At school
you practice protective coloration,
dress like headbangers who look so tough-
skinned no one messes with them.

At home you're each other's safer targets,
but when I hear a scream and find one
of you writhing from a well-aimed kick,
I feel the jab beneath my ribs
in a spot permanently tender.

And when one of you runs in, blood running
down his temple from a wound inflicted
by his brother, I recall the painted dinosaurs
we saw at the Natural History Museum: twin males
butting heads like mountain kids that furor made
one two-headed, eight-limbed, two-tailed monster.

The legend said the ten-inch dome of solid bone
transferred the impact of a blow through the neck
and back to spare the small brain a concussion.
Their mother isn't watching, and if she saw
she wouldn't recognize the pair bashing heads
as her hatchlings. Her pelvis never felt this
twinge of witness, this weighty memory
of still-soft skulls sliding from her
on the blood's red carpet. She never knew
this new species of pain.

Love Letter from My Son

I wanted to be a missionary;
he wants to be a mercenary.

He knows when I feed birds
I want something in return—

rubies on the finch's rump and throat.
To him it looks like blood.

This morning I forgot
to sprinkle seed over the snow.

Home from work I see the silver
maple tree studded with finches

and below, a mound of seed
to feed the multitudes.

He won't admit to the deed, but I see
his sneakers' prints from door to tree,

and it's as if he's hung
my neck in jewels

or in the letter he writes with his life
he's changed *mercenary* to *mercy*,

the mound outside a pardon of the world
and of me, the woman who feeds him.

WOMEN WHO DREAM OF MEN

When I was leaving my first husband
whose great red mane had fallen
under morphine's pillow, I dreamed
I was playing pool with my grandfather.
Four punks chased us from the basement
onto city bricks. I held his hand
and ran, remembering he'd died
of a heart attack. It was giving
out again. He had to stop.
I didn't, and let go of his hand.

I tell my mother, his daughter,
this dream, crying. *You're all right,*
she says, *don't cry,* soothing me
as she did when as a child I woke
gasping. *That wasn't Grandpa.*
That was John (my husband).

Years later I fall in love
with the man who would succeed him,
at least partly for his hands—
long and slender like my grandfather's.
The first summer when he was away fishing
I kept seeing Grandpa's fingers
on his fishing rod, the last thing
on earth he ever touched.

When my husband is dying
in my dream, I ask if he would like
to see the stars one last time.
I support his weight to the back door,
his wrestler's body graceful still,

a sleek, wounded gazelle. The door
opens onto the yard where I was twelve.
It's cold and we are lucky.
Stars have never been so near.

Chilled, I wake and press my body
into his curled back. His skin
feels new against my breasts and belly.
I don't remember when I touched it last.
In the morning I tell him the dream.
He says my love—long in hibernation—
is finally waking. I can't seem to wake
from the dream. When I tell my mother,
she says *you're afraid your love*
for him is dying.

When she had three teenaged girls
sleeping under her roof, wild beasts
stalked the jungle of her sleep,
one of us always the helpless prey.
Night after night she saved us
who could not escape without her.

Beside her my father sleeps
deep as a fisherman's hook buried
beneath a generation's drifted silt,
bringing nothing to the surface
on its sharp tooth.

To a Serious Woman

Reading the Postcard Painting

for Judy

When you sent the card, did you know
you were the willow stretching
to touch where we begin?
Two of your slender limbs
dip into the water near your trunk.

I wonder if you meant for me
to be the water lily
whose face opens beneath you
petal by white petal
as if by invitation.
Although the water doesn't mention it,
the green mountain behind us
sulks alone in its mists, upholding
the notion of distance even here.

THE BLUE HOUR

for Linnea, who sent me three cards

1. *Haystacks, Setting Sun*

Light taking leave of these haystacks,
painting their snow-glazing blue, pulls
me backward through a thousand sunsets
to my mother's kitchen where she might be
pulling muffins drizzled with white icing
from her oven lit by pink light
pressing through the window.

Westbound on I-80, leaving Nebraska,
I saw these haystacks in blue light
as I left behind the rolling torso
of the land, the forms you saw as rising
quickbreads, women's breasts, offering
the lone eye nourishment: signs of love
along that stretch of highway.

2. *A Summer Evening along Skagen Svenderstrand*

Once an artist told me twilight
was the hardest time to capture—
only a flicker's muted blush of underwing
taking flight the moment it's discovered,
its dusty rouge lighting the heart
before the eye can hunt it.

Here, in the split second when sky
and sea agree to take one hue, two

women trail gauze gowns laced with sea foam
across sand. Their steps leave pockets
of blue light the sea will slip
its hands into, reclaim. But first
these two friends will have their moment,
heads inclining toward a secret blooming
in blue light between their faces.

3. *Reading by Lamplight*

Now comes the darker twilight, the violet
panel between parted curtains, the time
of night the heart's most full of longing,
most watchful for another heart to fill it:
when my mother's beauty hovered
between everyday and exquisite. Changing
for evening, she highlighted cheekbones
with pink powder and painted black arches
over her eyes. When did day turn to night?
While I was watching her eyes
closing and the deep blue shadow
stroked across her eyelids.

This woman is alone, though, at her table,
and I try to guess what friend, what love,
she's missing. But her profile of attention
says she's traveled a long way to reach
this quiet. Perhaps she likes
that the frilly lamp she's brought in
from the dresser can't cast its dim

light on everything—not on her face, her plain
dress, or the room's few furnishings: only
her wrist and fingers holding her book open,
turning light from page to page
past nightfall.

FROM THE ART MUSEUM'S ORIENTAL WING

for Kris

Any mirror would say you're a Vermeer
and not a watercolor courtesan,
but I can see your slender feet
tucked beneath your kneeling form
before this writing box, its bridges
stretching across waves etched deeply
as furrows in the fields where we grew up.
Beside it, a bronze water holder ripens
to the green and rose-gold fitted
to its shape—a juicy pear.

Something of woman here.
Perhaps an empress penned love
poems across the grain, or composed
sorrow into the accepted forms:
crane, mountain, cherry blossom.
You might write of the scene:
stems reach up from a gnarled branch
to unmarred ebony, its hidden promise.
Inside it, nothing but a stone,
but all you need: something for characters
to sit on, stumble over, and more
undernourished branches. I swear
they reach for nothing.

We balance one another: grounded
stone and gold-dust clouds.
First one believes in marriage,
then the other; one marries,

and the other leaves her husband.
But neither one is willing to forego
the love-play hinted at in breeze-stirred
silk sheers of this testered bed.
No wonder we keep falling
for its soft down pleasures,
its many-pillowed drowse, opium-potent.

I'm ready now to try on the tiara
of April-morning-blue kingfisher feathers
covering a perforated fretwork,
but the sign tells me the popularity
of this bird's plumage led to her extinction,
that the feathers quiver if brushed by wind
or wearer's movement, as if still
attached to life and torment.

Life, yes, and even torment
if we choose it. But another woman
chose these lotus slippers, chose
to have her toe and sole bones broken
and reshaped to four-inch crescents.
Woman? No, a girl of eight, her blood
just learning to obey the moon.

A pair of sixteenth century handscrolls
rolls out the story we know
like the back of our own handwork.
The warrior Isozake brings home
a second wife, which naturally
drives the first wife crazy.

She puts on the next face
in her repertoire—the grinning demon—
and beats to death her younger
self, her rival, with a staff.
Both staff and mask adhere to her
until she takes vows and shaves her head.

If you were here we'd argue
which is worse: vows or a shaved head,
agree that he deserved the demon
treatment, not his sweetie.
But, dear friend, are we unbiased
judges, having ourselves bared
polished teeth over a man?

The last painting, from our century,
retells with new details the ancient story:
a modern Chinese beauty leans into blood-
crimson for the sake of contrast. It's
breathtaking. She leans to see more clearly
in her mirror the imaginary line
her hand must follow, leans,
I fear, into the blinding
point of her eye pencil.

To a Serious Woman

You are a serious woman who laughs
and raises a daughter alone.
But when the poems don't come
or the support checks
or the calls answering your calls
you wonder what it all means.

We bring out crystal
for wine on my front porch.
Our children pass noisily
before us on the sidewalk,
popsicles and hot wheels, my sons
competing for your daughter's
single-hearted love. *Where are the men
to equal us?* we rave and shake our heads.

We agree that it's enough
on these long front porch nights
to let the summer dusk collect
along the edges of our talk,
laughter a haze around the moon.

When I leave my lover,
you offer a way to pass uncut
through the sharpened blades
of the first night alone.
Buy a bottle of wine, you say,
put on some Joni Mitchell,
sit down at your dining room table
with your work and say this:

This is my home.
This is my work.
This is my life.

I hypnotize myself through
twenty-one nights with this mantra,
but when I call you the next night
from his studio, a lapsed believer,
you say: Tell him to take a leap.
I don't, and later you forgive me
when I tell you that after loving him
that night I left him in my bed
and bore testimony before stars
on my back porch, repeating over
and over like Hail Marys:

This is my home.
This is my work.
This is my life.

Now you have a decision to make.
A serious one, so we drink and drink.
Should you and your daughter
leave all this for work
you've been offered in the east?
I say go, choose growth,
knowing it will find you here
or there whether or not you choose it.

So we drink some more
and the night falls

heavy as our children's lives
around our shoulders.
Too much night and wine now
for words, but we both know
that our lives are better
for the lovers we leave or appease,
for other places calling us,
for children to tuck into silence
between cool, dark sheets.

This is my home.
This is my work.
This is my life.

JUDITH MICKEL SORNBERGER

Judith Mickel Sornberger lives in Mansfield, Pennsylvania, with her husband, writer Bruce Barton, and is the mother of adult twin sons. An Assistant Professor of English and Director of the Women's Studies Program at Mansfield University, she received her Ph.D., M.A., and B.A. from the University of Nebraska-Lincoln. She was born in Omaha, Nebraska.

Ms. Sornberger's publications include *CALYX, A Journal of Art and Literature by Women, Prairie Schooner, Kalliope, Tar River Poetry, The Laurel Review, West Branch, Yarrow, Puerto del Sol, Sing Heavenly Muse, Nebraska Humanities*, and *Denver Quarterly*. She is one of five poets published in *Adjoining Rooms* (Platte Valley Press, 1985), and she edited *All My Grandmothers Could Sing/ Poems by Nebraska Women* (Free Rein Press, 1984). Her essays and poetry are also published in *Sexual Harassment: Women Speak Out* (The Crossing Press, 1992) and *Mother to Daughter/Daughter to Mother* (The Feminist Press, 1984), edited by Tillie Olsen.

Her awards include a Presidential Fellowship from the University of Nebraska, an AAUW Graduate Fellowship, the Vreeland Award for Poetry, an Academy of American Poets Award, and the Oldfield Fine Arts Scholarship. She held a residency at the Cottages at Hedgebrook (Whidbey Island, WA).

Selected Titles from Award-Winning CALYX Books

The Violet Shyness of Their Eyes: Notes from Nepal, by Barbara J. Scot. A moving account of a western woman's transformative sojourn in Nepal as she reaches mid-life. *(Nov. 1993)*
ISBN 0-934971-35-8, $12.95, paper; ISBN 0-934971-36-6, $22.95, cloth.

Raising the Tents, by Frances Payne Adler. A personal and political volume of poetry, documenting a woman's discovery of her voice. Finalist, 1993 WESTAF Book Awards.
ISBN 0-934971-33-1, $9.95, paper; ISBN 0-934971-34-x, $19.95, cloth.

Killing Color, by Charlotte Watson Sherman. These compelling, mythical short stories by a gifted storyteller delicately explore the African-American experience. 1992 GLCA New Writers Fiction Award.
ISBN 0-934971-17-X, $9.95, paper; ISBN 0-934971-18-8, $19.95, cloth.

Mrs. Vargas and the Dead Naturalist, by Kathleen Alcalá. Fourteen stories set in Mexico and the Southwestern U.S., written in the tradition of magical realism.
ISBN 0-934971-25-0, $9.95, paper; ISBN 0-934971-26-9, $19.95, cloth.

Black Candle, by Chitra Divakaruni. Lyrical and honest poems that chronicle significant moments in the lives of South Asian women. 1993 Gerbode Award.
ISBN 0-934971-23-4, $9.95, paper; ISBN 0-934971-24-2, $19.95 cloth.

Ginseng and Other Tales from Manila, by Marianne Villanueva. Poignant short stories set in the Philippines. 1992 Manila Critic's Circle National Literary Award Nominee.
ISBN 0-934971-19-6, $9.95, paper; ISBN 0-934971-20-X, $19.95, cloth.

Idleness Is the Root of All Love, by Christa Reinig, translated by Ilze Mueller. These poems by the prize-winning German poet accompany two older lesbians through a year together in love and struggle.
ISBN 0-934971-21-8, $10, paper; ISBN 0-934971-22-6, $18.95, cloth.

The Forbidden Stitch: An Asian American Women's Anthology, edited by Shirley Geok-lin Lim, et. al. The first Asian American women's anthology. Winner of the American Book Award.
ISBN 0-934971-04-8, $16.95, paper; ISBN 0-934971-10-2, $32, cloth.

Women and Aging, An Anthology by Women, edited by Jo Alexander, et. al. The only anthology that addresses ageism from a feminist perspective. A rich collection of older women's voices.
ISBN 0-934971-00-5, $15.95, paper; ISBN 0-934971-07-2, $28.95, cloth.

In China with Harpo and Karl, by Sibyl James. Essays revealing a feminist poet's experiences while teaching in Shanghai, People's Republic of China.
ISBN 0-934971-15-3, $9.95, paper; ISBN 0-934971-16-1, $17.95, cloth.

Indian Singing in 20th Century America, by Gail Tremblay. A work of hope by a Native American poet.
ISBN 0-934971-13-7, $9.95, paper; ISBN 0-934971-14-5, $19.95, cloth.

Forthcoming Titles – 1994

Light in the Crevice Never Seen, by Haunani-Kay Trask. The first book of poetry by an indigenous Hawaiian woman to be published on the mainland.
ISBN 0-934971-37-4, $9.95, paper; ISBN 0-934971-38-2, $19.95, cloth.

CALYX Books is committed to producing books of literary, social, and feminist integrity.

These books are available at your local bookstore or direct from:

CALYX Books, PO Box B, Corvallis, OR 97339

(Please include payment with your order. Add $1.50 postage for first book and $.75 for each additional book.)

*CALYX, Inc., is a nonprofit organization
with a 501(C)(3) status.
All donations are tax deductible.*

Colophon

The text of Open Heart *was set in Caslon 540. Section pages and cover type appears in Caslon Open Face.*

Design and typeset by ImPrint Services, Corvallis, Oregon.